A REPRINT OF

THOMAS EWING DABNEY'S "OCEAN SPRINGS: THE LAND WHERE DREAMS COME TRUE" (CIRCA 1915) (A photographic essay on life in Ocean Springs, Mississippi)

About the author: Thomas Ewing Dabney, 1885 - 1970, was truly a "Renaissance Man".

He, for his lifetime, had a distinguished career as a reporter, editor, author, adventurer, lecturer, Shakespearian expert, legislator, service club prexy (Rotary, Lions, C. of C.); high honors in Masonry (Grand Consistory of Louisiana, Friends of Harmony Lodge 58, F&AM, and St. John Royal Arch Lodge F&AM); active in the Episcopal Church. A graduate of Sewanee, University of the South, he was the first Southern college graduate to obtain a master's degree from Harvard in one year, where he was a scholarship student. His interest in higher education was continued in New Mexico, where he served as a Regent for the N. M. School of Mines, and lecturer in journalism at the Un. of N. M.

"Tom" Dabney was the son of Dr. Thomas Smith Dabney, whose early methods of treating yellow fever became textbook teaching. It was after he contracted malaria while serving as temporary chargé d'affaires in the U.S. Embassy in Mexico that he came to Ocean Springs in 1912.

Here he developed the pecan orchards and had a dairy farm at the place called "The Field" on Lover's Lane. His children spent much of their youth at that place.

Among his tremendous literary output were his books: "Tropic Intrigue" "Revolution or Jobs" "The Man Who Bought the Waldorf" and the award-winning "One Hundred Great Years" - history of the Times Picayune.

In 1907 he married lovely Winifred Michaels of London, England, and they had four children. "Winnie" did not survive Tom by many months. Their children are David Dabney, Mrs. Pat D. Bush and Mrs. Dorothy D. Kehoe, and Mrs. Natalie D. Arnold.

Tom Dabney's tremendous literary files will become the property of Tulane University library, available to scholars and historians.

The 1699 Historical Committee is grateful to Tom Dabney's children for permission to republish this book. They stipulate that any profits from its sale will be used by this committee to perpetuate the history of Ocean Springs.

Foreword by:
Delores Davidson Smith, Historian
Book Chairman; Mark Watson

The spot we call Ocean Springs was the nucleus of a nation, and neither the Massachusetts nor the Virginia settlements could exceed in importance the wondrous results with which Iberville's ships were laden when he sailed into Back Bay in the winter of 1699, built the fort on the high bluff north of where the L. & N. Railroad bridge now is, and founded the first Caucasion colony planted by the French in their new world possessions of the South. Ocean Springs became the capital of the vast Louisiana Territory, with New Orleans for one of its dependencies.

But Iberville was too blinded by thoughts of gold to see what a wondrous agricultural region this was. He found Indians among whom want and destitution had never been known, but even that did not tell him. He named this place Biloxi in honor of the Indians. He found a region lofty, with natural drainage, and a natural health resort—E-Ca-Na-Cha-Hah, or Holy Ground, the Indians called the section now known as the "Point," and they came from hundreds of miles to drink the Sacred Waters of our medicinal springs.

It was a later generation that found the gold Iberville could not see—the golden apples of mythology; the gold that grows on trees. As Ocean Springs was the foundation of a new country in the seventeenth century, so it is the cradle of a new industry in the twentieth.

The people who come here to visit expect to find only a pleasant place of sojourn—a region free from malaria, a panacea for consumption, asthma, catarrah, neuralgia, rheumatism, and intestinal troubles; a natural cure for hay fever; where the water is of the purest, hospitality of the finest, and life of the easiest; where there are no extremes of heat, cold, or rain; where instead of blizzards we have roses; and where the breezes, now touched with the aroma of the pines, now laden with the vigor of the sea, forever work their miracles.

But they stay! They stay! They see orange trees with twenty dollars of fruit on them. They see pecan trees bringing greater returns than rented houses, with nuts selling wholesale at one cent each. They

see our persimmons first on the market.
They see oranges and grapefruit, three
years old, yield the highest priced fruit
in the United States—and the supply
never equal to the demand. They see
men reaping astonishing profits from
papershell pecan trees, planted when
they were fifty years old.

And they stay! They stay to be near
the sea, to enjoy the fish and oysters, to
play golf and pick flowers when the rest
of the world is snow-weary!

And year by year, as they increase
their orchards, they send for their
friends, they wax great in health,
wealth, and happiness.

HEALTHY FOR CHILDREN

A LAW ABIDING TOWN

The first thing that strikes the visitor is the utter absence of anything
approaching a race problem or race questions in Ocean Springs. There
is no part of town in which a lady with modesty or safety can not go.
Friction between the races, there is none; and none of the violence which
is reported in other communities, although twenty-five percent of the population is black.

One reason for this almost unique state of affairs, is found in the efforts of Thos. I. Keys, the colored leader of Ocean Springs. Mr. Keys,
who served as postmaster under Harrison, McKinley, Roosevelt, and Ttaft
—a term of officec extending over twenty years—is an educated man and
is devoting himself to the uplift of his people, and teaching them to live
honorably and proudly. For the past five years Mr. Keys has been con-
ducting a successful general store.

OFF FOR A DAY'S HUNT.   GEO. DALE FOLLOWING HIS POINTERS

George Dale, in addition to being the leading plumber and sheet iron
worker of Ocean Springs, is a crack shot and an ardent sportsman.   To
everybody who knows George, and shoots behind his dogs, this is the Happy
Hunting Grounds.

Partridges, doves, snipe, ducks, woodcocks, turkeys, rabbits, 'possum,
and deer are found.   The quail hunting on the cut-over pine lands is the
favorite sport.   The birds are found even in the town limits, and five
miles is the furthest that one needs go.

ORCHARD HOMES OF OCEAN SPRINGS

Reading downward, in natural order: S. C. Spencer, Mrs. Tom Chase, J. C. Akeley, "Sunny Ridge Farm," W. W. Grinstead, of Gautier, Miss, and Newton Jones.

THE BUSY CORNER OF OCEAN SPRINGS

**Showing the Ocean Springs State Bank,, the Ocean Springs Drug Store,
the Postoffice, and the Telephone Exchange, the latter upstairs.**

The Ocean Springs State Bank, which is the oldest financial institution here, was founded in 1905.   Prosperity followed its inception, and in a few years, it was forced to vacate its original quarters and build its present handsome brick home.

The building, including the postoffice annex, has been entirely paid for by the profits of the Bank, which never has had to re-discount a note, and which has always paid dividends as regular as the interest on Government bonds.

Dr. O. L. Bailey is the President, and is a strong believer in the orchard possibilities of this region.   Dr. Bailey is developing orchard properties himself.

The capital and surplus amount to $25,000, deposits, $125,000; resources, $150,000.

In the Ocean Springs Drug Store, you are sure to meet your friends. The building is cool, a special power plant supplies lights and fans, and every effort is made to make the stranger feel at home.

------o------

THE SATSUMA ORANGE

This juicy, tender, delicious orange is a fortune in itself.   It is seedless, vigorous and hardy, successfully withstanding every climatic condition in the temperatures of the Gulf Coast.   It is the hardiest of all varieties of the orange family, and in a dormant condition will stand a temperature of from 12 to 14 degrees above zero—from 10 to 15 degrees lower than the ordinary orange.

It shows considerable fruiting at three years old, and after the fourth year, will run from two boxes up per tree per annum, with an increased production as the trees grow.   There are trees in this section that show a fruiting of 3,000 oranges to the tree.

The natural growth of the Satsuma Orange tree is bushy; the trees hardly ever exceed eight feet in height, which is an advantage in gathering the fruit, as ladders and scaffoldings are unnecessary.   The trees are entirely free from thorns.   The fruit is eaten at any time, or place, easily and safely from soiling apparel or fingers, or losing one single drop of the juice.

The Satsuma is a money maker because:

1.   It is in a class by itself, and there is no other orange that has the flavor or sweetness that this little orange has.

2.   This orange is an early producer, bearing a commercial crop the third year from planting.

3.   Being an early orange, it is ripened on the trees, from October 25th to November 25th, and the fruit can all be on the market before Christmas, before danger of any low temperature catching the fruit on the tree and damaging the fruit, as is the case with the Florida and Louisiana orange.

FARMERS AND MERCHANTS STATE BANK

Because of the rapid growth of Ocean Springs, the Farmers & Merchants State Bank was formed in February, 1913.   Its directors are leading business men of the community, who believe in the future of this region and who encourage by every means in their power the development of citrus and pecan orchards.

Chas. E. Pabst, the well known orchardist and nurseryman, to whose discovery is due the astonishing pecan industry, is very appropriately, the President of the Farmers & Merchants State Bank.

As it is a Guaranty Fund Bank, it offers the public every possible protection.   Deposits amount to $200,000.

The building, which is a handsome brick edifice, is situated in the most commanding part of town, opposite Marshall Park, and facing the depot. It is the first sight that greets the stranger's eye.

AUTO DELIVERY OF THE EAGLE POINT OYSTER COMPANY.
A. P. KOTZUM, PROPRIETOR.

The seafoods constitute one of the greatest attractions Ocean Springs has to offer.   Fish are uncommonly plentiful, and the oysters are unsurpassed.

The oyster industry of the Coast represents a two million dollar business; but the product of our canneries can not be compared with the exquisite flavor of the bivalves eaten fresh from the water.

Nowhere on the Coast are the oysters finer than those of Ocean Springs, as everyone will acknowledge after sampling the oysters of the Eagle Point Oyster Company.

RESIDENCE OF FRANK H. BRYAN

One of the modern homes of Ocean Springs, located on one of the principal avenues and fronting the beach.   He is now developing one of the finest pecan and grape fruit orchards hereabouts.

Views on the E. S. Perryman Estate.   Breaking ground, Residence.
Poultry Yard, Mrs. Perryman and her famous dogs, the Aviary.

FISHING

As Ocean Springs lies on Fort Bayou and the Mississippi Sound, both fresh and salt water fishing are provided. Because of the brackish water, it is the rule rather than the exception, to catch fresh water fish along with the denizens of the Gulf. The Northern tourist early discovers that the artificial fly, on a warm day in January, is equally alluring to the bass, the pike, the redfish, and the speckled trout.

Other salt water fish: Croakers, mullet, white trout, speckled trout, are plentiful. Spanish mackeral abound nearby, and there are frequent excursions to the famous snapper banks. And then there is the mighty tarpon, if you care to pit your skill against the might of the silver king!

Here are some fishing records made off Ocean Springs during the past year: 4-pound speckled trout, by Charlie Dryden, the well known sports writer, who makes his winter home in Ocean Springs.

140-Pound sea bass caught by Charlie Ryan, near Ocean Springs. Length, 5 feet; 20 inches wide, 10 inches thick

M. P. Julian, of New Orleans, caught 150 fish in a morning's sport at the L. & N. Railroad bridge. D. Ross Metzger, of New Orleans, hooked and caught a 22-pound redfish at the same place, measuring 39¾ inches in length. John Wirth and Chas. Bacher, of New Orleans, caught 80 fish before breakfast. The same anglers a little before, landed 500 in a morning's sport. B. H. Hammond and Dr. Edward Reinhart of Columbus, Ohio, caught 46 speckled trout, weighing 93 pounds, dressed, in a morning's sport in Fort Bayou. Willie Dale caught a 9½ pound flounder.

The L. & N. bridge mentioned is in Ocean Springs. Some of the best fishing is at the Fort Bayou bridge, two blocks from the post office, and here in the town limits some astonishing records are hung up.

A MORNING'S SPORT

S. Leonard Boyce, a Chicago attorney, kept an elaborate system of records during the winter of 1915 here on the Gulf Coast and showed that the temperature of the water ranged from 60 to 65 degrees. All through the winter he went in swimming in the Bay.

Residence of J. H. Behrens, "Terrace Hill"

FORT BAYOU FRUIT COMPANY

One of the promising concerns in the outlying districts of Ocean Springs is the Fort Bayou Fruit Company, located about nine miles northeast of town.

The company was formed in 1909, and is made up mostly of people from Chicago and the surrounding country.   They acquired a hundred acres of land and immediately set to work clearing and developing it. Having spent the first year in civilizing the land, they planted during the fol'owing winter, 750 of the best grafted pecan trees, 2200 satsuma orange trees, 300 grapefruit trees and 300 Japanese Persimmons.

The trees have received good care and are promising a big crop for next fall.

As an adjunct to the fruit growing business, trucking and stock raising is being carried on quite extensively and the enterprise bears every evidence of success.

The officers of the company are J. H. Behrens, President and Manager, Ocean Springs, Miss.; Parker A. Jenks, Vice-President, and John Vennema, Secretary, both of Chicago, Ill.

A. C. GOTTSCHE'S MODERN GROCERY STORE

————o————

Home, orchard and nursery of John P. Edwards, one of the leading developers of Ocean Springs. Mr. Edwards is opening some of the most desirable land in this region to colonization.

The Garrard Hardware Store, With Auto Delivery

The exclusive Hardware Store of Ocean Springs, it contains a stock that one would expect in a city five times the size. It is operated by Mrs. Joseph .B Garrard.

Mrs. Garrard's residence, Bayou Home, is one of the handsomest in Ocean Springs, as will be seen from its photograph on another page.

Mrs. Garrard is just as successful in developing the Ben-Jim Orchards, and is unable to supply the demand for Satsumas and grapefruit.

HANDSOME HOMES OF OCEAN SPRINGS

Reading downward in natural order: Mrs. D. V. Purington, Mrs. Joseph Kotzum, Mrs. Emma Besore, T. E. Dabney, Dr. G. M. Melvin, E. S. Davis, H. H. Germain. Note the height of green peas back of M. D. Busey.

GATHERING GOLDEN NUGGETS IN SUNSHINE LAND

An orchard scene near Ocean Springs, which, according to G. A. Park, General Immigration and Industrial Agent of the L. & N. Railroad, is "in the lead of any other section on our road for citrus fruit."

Jackson county produced in 1915, 10,000 straps or 12 cars of satsuma oranges, worth $20,000. They sold for $4 and up per box (or strap), the highest priced citrus produced in the United States. It is the earliest variety on the market, and the best.

HANDSOME HOMES OF OCEAN SPRINGS
Reading downward, in natural order: Dr. Wm. Porter, J. A. Witty, Capt. Charles B. McVay, Alfred Bonnabel, Minor Russell, Major F. M. Weed.

MARSHALL PARK

------o------

OCEAN SPRINGS CIVIC FEDERATION

That civic life and the aim for "The Beautiful" are active in our town. is well demonstrated by the work of the Civic Federation.

From a very small beginning in the spring of 1911, this organization has worked itself up so as to be now considered one of the institutions of the city. Realizing that there was room for improvement in many directions. the members at first confined their efforts to the establishment of a public park. A suitable piece of land was found near the railroad depot, and the idea of transforming this into a park met with a ready response from the public, so that sufficient funds were raised to begin work, and with aid from the L. & N. Railroad, it was made possible to create what is now known as Marshall Park.

In the course of time, many improvements have been made, a bandstand and sanitary fountain have been added, and with the beautiful shrubbery and walks, it presents a pleasing invitation to the town.

There are many other evidences around town, testifying to the fact that there is a silent, but persistent force, working for The Uplift, and that this force for civic improvement is supported by public opinion.

SUGAR CANE

Sugar cane is grown for syrup manufacturing throughout this section of the Gulf Coast, and for quality of syrup and tonnage of cane grown per acre, no part of the cane growing sections surpass Jackson County. The planting of the cane is done usually once in every two or four years, after the first year planting, the following two or three crops are grown from the same roots or stubble. Under ordinary conditions, the average production can be relied on being 20 tons per acre, or 400 gallons of pure high-grade syrup per acre, selling readily at 40 to 65 cents per gallon.

Sunstrokes are unheard of here; horses are not stricken as in the North, our flowers are blooming while snow is shrouding the earth elsewhere.

A DISTINGUISHED GROUP OWNING ORCHARDS HERE

Left to right: Senator Wm. H. Maclean, of Chicago; Mrs. I. H. Snell, I. H. Snell, Mrs. Maclean, S. G. Gilfillan, of Ironton, O.

WHY PEOPLE COME TO OCEAN SPRINGS

Senator Vardaman was heard to say on a recent visit to Ocean Springs: "Nothing would suit me better than to live here."

"I have been to California and don't consider that as an orchard proposition, or as a place to live in, it can be mentioned in the same breath with this Coast."—Senator Wm. H. Maclean.

1915.

"It is immediately apparent to the newcomer that Ocean Springs has a present opportunity and a wonderful future. It has several of the best natural advantages of any point on the Gulf Coast. It needs no artificial aid to beauty and attractiveness.."—H. F. Miller, Mgr. Chicago Chamber of Com.

"I chose the Coast because it is the best country; I chose Ocean Springs because it is the nicest and most progressive town on the Coast."— Dr. G. M. Melvin.   "It is our opinion that the Ocean Springs climate is rather the finest in the world.   We were almost frozen on that French Riviera in April of 1914."— Francis Cropper.   Emerson Hough, the noted writer, said: "I make Ocean Springs my winter home because this is the finest spot on the Coast.   The hunting is fine, the fishing is splendid, and the fellowship is unsurpassed."

HALSTEAD & SONS NURSERY AND ORCHARDS

Halstead & Sons are also among the reliable orchardists and nurserymen on our Coast.   E. W. Halstead, former Assistant Horticulturist for the Island of Cuba, is in charge, and they have attained great successes under his management, with the most popular varieties of Pecan trees, as well as with the Satsuma and grapefruit.   They are firm believers in rootgrafting.   The work of the son, E. W. Halstead, for five years in charge of horticultural work in New Mexico and for ten years in Cuba, in building some of the largest citrus orchards in the island, one being of 2,000 acres, gave him valuable experience in successful orchard development, and building.

NUT IMPORTATIONS
Showing the Increasing Demand
Government Bureau of Statistics, Washington, D. C.

1901	$3,056,137	1906	$7,228,607
1902	$4,214,676	1907	$9,315,891
1903	$5,038,726	1908	$9,563,742
1904	$5,473,306	1909	13,246,667
1905	$6,154,515	1911	14,497,435

LOOKING SEAWARD FROM THE E. S. PERRYMAN EAST BEACH HOME.
MR. AND MRS. PERRYMAN IN THE FOREGROUND

Bay Wiew

Pecan Nursery

C. F. Forkert,

Proprietor.

BULLETIN NO. 251; U. S. DEPARTMENT OF AGRICULTURE:

"The Pecan is the most important of the nut bearing trees now grown in the United States." Of all the wealth producing members of the nut family, the paper shell pecan is king. The nuts find ready market at from 60c to $1 a pound although at 25c a pound the profit to the grower would be enormous.

LUTHER BURBANK, THE GREATEST LIVING HORTICULTURIST:

"Speaking of the pecan, we must dismiss the idea of ever over-producing the pecan. We have not one pecan where we ought to have a million to create a market. The immense earning capacity and longevity of pecan orchards make them the most profitable and permanent investment of anything in the agricultural line."

A WAGONLOAD OF WEALTH

C. S. Bell, the well known nurseryman and orchardist of Ocean Springs, is filling an order.   The picture was snapped in front of the bank, which is the most appropriate setting imaginable.   The shipment consists of 2719 pounds of choice paper shell nuts, contained in 33 sacks and 5 barrels.

Mr. Bell planted his pecan orchard when he was fifty years old.   From 200 trees, 10 years old, he gathered 4,700 pounds of fancy nuts in the 1915 season, which wholesaled for 35 cents a pound, bringing nearly

THE MODERN BAKERY AND RESIDENCE OF FRANK E. SCHMIDT

$2,000, or 10 percent on $1,000 an acre.   The hay sold from the orchard more than paid the expense of making the crop.

The Jackson County pecan crop of 1915 brought $100,000.   Records like Mr. Bell's prove how quickly and profitably the trees come in bearing.

Another resident of Jackson County in 1901 grafted a pecan tree at a cost of $1; at the same time he built 5 houses, to rent at $5 each, for $1,200.   In the succeeding fourteen years he received more actual profit from the $1 invested in a pecan tree than in the $1,299 invested in houses!

C. F. White, of Ocean Springs, has the same story to tell.   From 270 12-year old pecan trees he sold last year (1915) 3,400 pounds of fancy pecans, which brought over $1,000, or better than 10 percent on $10,000. Mr. White is also a shipper of Satsumas, as he has 125 splendid three-year old trees.   His orchard home is a beauty, and his success shows what a city man, without any previous training, can have.

STORE OF E. S. DAVIS & SONS, FOUNDED 1883

The leading mercantile establishment of Ocean Springs, it typifies the growth of this region.

After working several years for his brother, G. W. Davis, (now dead) E. S. Davis went into partnership with him in 1878.   The brothers had a small store on the site of the present Lundy Building, opposite the Ocean Springs State Bank.

In 1883 they bought and built on their present location.   The building was only 30x50 feet, and the stock hardly amounted to $3,000.

Every year since there has been some new addition or improvement. At first it was the building that was enlarged.   Its size now is 60x120 feet.

A few months ago an auto delivery was installed.

As Ocean Springs grew, so did the store of E. S. Davis grow.   And as this climate and soil will produce practically anything under the sun, so you can supply every need from the enormous stock of this store.

Mr. Davis, who is one of the most progressive men in the community, is director of the Farmers & Merchants State Bank, a stockholder in the Ocean Springs State Bank, and a stockholder in the Builders Supply Co. He supports everything that goes to develop Ocean Springs.

Views on Shore Acres, the famous estate of Mrs. A. L. Benjamin.   One
of the handsomest homes in the entire South.

Shore Acres.   The Estate contains 50 acres; has a water frontage of three-quarters of a mile; and one mile of Schillinger driveways.

CHAS. E. PABST

No book on Ocean Springs or pecan culture would be complete without a reference to Chas. E. Pabst, the proprietor of the famous Ocean Springs Nursery. To Mr. Pabst is directly due the paper shell pecan industry, for he is the first man who made a successful graft in a pecan tree.

The discovery reads like one of the wildest feats of romance. No one had ever been able to propagate a nut except by layering. Planting fine specimens did not produce results true to seed. Mr. Pabst reasoned it out thus grafting was possible.

Everybody told him that he was foredoomed to failure. But still he continued to experiment, using his scanty savings for the purpose. There came a time when even he despaired. But he determined to make one more attempt. This was in 1892. From 25 grafts, there were 13 successful results! The next season he put in 2100 grafts and got 23! But he knew he was right, and it was only a question of time for him to perfect the method.

Mr. Pabst, starting out as a laborer a few years ago, has developed one of the most remarkable orchards in the United States. The proposition was recently made to him to capitalize the property for $100,000, he to remain in charge, and retain $51,000 for his share. Mr. Pabst refused.

Showing how land has appreciated in value, because of his discovery it may be mentioned that the price Mr. Pabst gave for his first nursery, was $1.50 an acre. After he started his nursery, he paid $27.50 for adjoining land. It is much higher now.

The pecan industry originated in Jackson County, almost in the town limits of Ocean Springs. This soil is simply ideal for pecans. The trees begin fruiting in the third and fourth year. There is abundant proof that the average bearing of a pecan tree—in a grove—is as follows:

6th year, 2 pounds; 7th year, 3 pounds; 8th year, 5 to 7 pounds; 9th year, 10 to 12 pounds; 10th year, 15 to 20 pounds, 11th year, 20 to 30 pounds; 12th year, 30 to 50 pounds and up.

After 12th year a tree would vary from 25 to 200 pounds per tree, with an average of say 40 to 50 pounds per tree per annum for the grove, figuring good and bad seasons during a series of years.

Mr. Pabst's nursery, which was started in 1896, is 20 acres in size and contains approximately 400,000 trees. In all he owns 120 acres.

Nine-year Old Pecan Grove of Chas. E. Pabst, of Ocean Springs, whose nursery stock is famous for its thriftiness.

Results on orchards like the above prove that the value of a pecan tree or a pecan grove cannot be over-estimated.   A single tree that will produce from $20 to $200 and more per annum is certainly worth some money.   The highest authorities state that a most conservative estimate of the increase in value of a pecan tree after transplanting is at least $5 per year

DUDLEY SCHEFFER

Another of the men who is doing so important an economic work for Ocean Springs is Dudley Scheffer.   As Mr. Pabst showed this region its opportunity, so Mr. Scheffer is advertising our possibilities throughout the length and breadth of the United States.

A land agent from the West, Mr. Scheffer came here several years ago, with all the enthusiasm and broadness of vision that one expects from that storied region.   In his development work, he has opened up several hundred acres to colonization, and has just secured an option on nearly two thousand more.   This land is being sold in tracts of five, ten, and fifteen acres; the number of families he is bringing to Sunshine Land, therefore, is easy of computation.

WINTER SCENE ON THE FAMOUS GRISWOLD PLACE

To the average person the results accomplished here seem fiction. There is, however, nothing unusual about them.

The two-acre tract of Mr. and Mrs. C. C. Griswold lies a mile and a half from Ocean Springs.   Three years ago (1912) when Mr. Griswold bought the property, it was under water.   A system of drainage made it habitable, and though Mr. Griswold was a city man, had never had experience in horticultural work, and was in ill health, by intensive methods he has made his two acres outyield the average ten.   They are yielding a handsome profit.

This is what you see on the Griswold place (besides chickens and the kitchen garden) 84 Satsuma orange trees, 51 grapefruit, 2 kumquats, 2 Kennedy lemons, 25 pecans, 2 persimmons, 2 figs, 1 plum, 5 pears, 1 peach, 2 apples, 2 scuppernongs and 12 bunch grape vines of standard varieties. The yield during the 1915 season was as follows:

Between two and three thousand oranges, six hundred and twenty grapefruit, nine dozen lemons, fourteen dozen peaches, (Albertas), one peck of apples and one hundred and thirty-three quarts of scuppernong grapes, and many pounds of bunch grapes, among them large white Niagara, which matures early and is of delicious flavor.

GLENGARIFF—RESIDENCE OF CAPTAIN FRANCIS O'NEILL

The kumquats, persimmons and figs gave quantities for table use and the pears were picked by bushels.

The pecan trees bore forty-five pounds of nuts.   One Stuart which was on the place, either five or six years old, bore three nuts in 1914, and this year (1915)) gave 19 pounds of selected nuts, running thirty-five to the pound three weeks after gathering them.

A Success tree, two and a half years old, bore four and a half pounds of very fine quality nuts.   Added to all this are 1,000 grafted pecan trees. A garden, strawberry bed, an up-to-date poultry house and two out-buildings, occupy the last remaining foot of land in the two acres and to plant even one thing more, something must be removed to make room for it.

STREET SCENES OF OCEAN SPRINGS.   SHADE AND FLOWERS ON EVERY HAND

TOWN RESIDENCE OF MR. AND MRS. THEODORE BECHTEL
FAMOUS FOR ITS FLOWERS

LEMON TREE AND BANANA PLANTS ON THE GROUNDS OF
THEODORE BECHTEL

An expert horticulturist, Mr. Bechtel delights to raise the most tropi-
cal fruits and flowers.

Mr. Bechtel owns Holcomb Boulevard, one of the finest orchards and
nurseries in the South.   Simply to see his thousands of orange and pecan
trees, is enough to make one wish to develop a grove.

Mr. Bechtel's Van Deman pecan tree holds the world's record. Planted in February, 1900, it began bearing in 1903, but no record was kept until 1910, from which time on, the figures are as follows:

Year	lbs.	Circumference inches	Spread feet	Year	lbs.	Circumference inches	Spread feet
				1912	70	40	40
				1913	185	45	45
1910	100	32	33	1914	85	50	48
1911	60	36	36	1915	183	54	52

Grafts from such trees as this, insure quick and profitable results.

Mr. Bechtel, a recognized expert in nut culture, is the introducer and propagator of the Success pecan, one of the best sellers on the market. It runs 40 to the pound. The price, wholesale, is 50 cents a pound.

Replying to the question, Is Pecan Orcharding a Profitable Investment, Mr. Bechtel answers emphatically, Yes. He adds: "But settle it for yourself by carefully estimating the yield per acre and the price at which choice pecans are now, or likely to be sold for some time to come, and you will see why we are putting every dollar we can command into pecan orchards. We think them very profitable at 25 cents per pound."

SCENE IN THE JAS. ASHWORTH ORCHARD

Mr. Ashworth is another city man without any previous experience, who has demonstrated what astonishing yields are possible from a small piece of ground. Four hundred and fifty dollars was his profit in 1915 from one acre of orange and pecan trees. His figures follow:

From 76 Satsuma trees, 8 years old, 6 grapefruit trees, 3 years old, and 13 papershell pecan trees, 2 Russells, and 4 seedlings, he sold:

30,000 oranges, at an average price of $8.80—Total, $264. (The 106 grapefruit were used in his own house, and are not considered here at all.) 1220 pecans, at 36 cents—$162; and 300 pounds of Russells and seedlings, $50—Total nuts and oranges, $476.

Less Expenses: Fertilizer, $14; spraying, $3.50; cultivation, $6; Labor, $3; Total, $26. Profit $450 per acre.

RESIDENCE OF GUSTAV HOTTINGER ON EAST BEACH

The Hottinger place was first laid out by the architect, Louis Sullivan, who built the great Auditorium Theatre and Hotel in Chicago about twenty-two years ago.

After enjoying his Southern home for a great many years, Mr. Sullivan sold the property to Gustav Hottinger, of Chicago, who delights to spend the winter here.   In his own words—"I think it the most restful place I could possibly go to, and the ideal spot to rest after the wear and tear of everyday life."

To all who love tropic beauty, the Hottinger place on East Beach is a riot of color and vegetation.   The rose garden is famous.   Vines, trees, and shubs shed their perfume on every hand.   The woodland walks winding through the property unfold beauty after beauty.

The house fronts the sea, and is one of the handsomest properties on the fashionable East Beach.

THE HOTTINGER ROSE GARDEN ON EAST BEACH

———o———

Lands sold in Jackson County ten years ago for $1.00 to $5.00 per acre, since it has been demonstrated that the pecan and satsuma orange are a success, are selling rapidly from $25 to $50 per acre, according to location.

ONE OF THE ORANGE GROVES BEING DEVELOPED BY M. R. HICKS

These trees are only two years transplanted and show a remarkab c growth, which is due to frequent cultivation.   Just three years ago this acreage was a wilderness of stumps, pines and palmetto.   The land was first thoroughly stumped by dynamite; broken up and limed and laid thus until the following year, when it was again plowed, disced and planted. Almost everything has been grown in between tree rows, strawberries, peanuts, peas, beans, garden truck, nursery stock, corn and even some cotton. The only fertilizing done was at time of planting intercrops, when only a light sprinkling in the furrows of a balanced fertilizer was used, and only enough to slightly change the soil texture.

Mr. Hicks has sold and developed, or sold and caused to be developed to pecans, oranges and grapefruit, nearly a thousand acres of land in the immediate vicinity of Ocean Springs the past three years.   The groves which range in size from one acre to forty, are owned by men and women of culture and refinement from various parts of the country, who will eventually make their homes here.

The firm of M. R. Hicks & Co., make a specialty of developed groves and care of orchards owned by non-residents.   A contract was recently closed for several hundred acres of the old Shannondale place, owned by Mr. Geo. E. McEwen, just two miles out on the County shell road, the north end of which for nearly a mile skirts beautiful old Fort Bayou.   This splendid acreage is named Bayou View Orchards and is being sub-divided and will shortly be sold and developed under contract on liberal terms.

REGATTA DAY OFF OCEAN SPRINGS

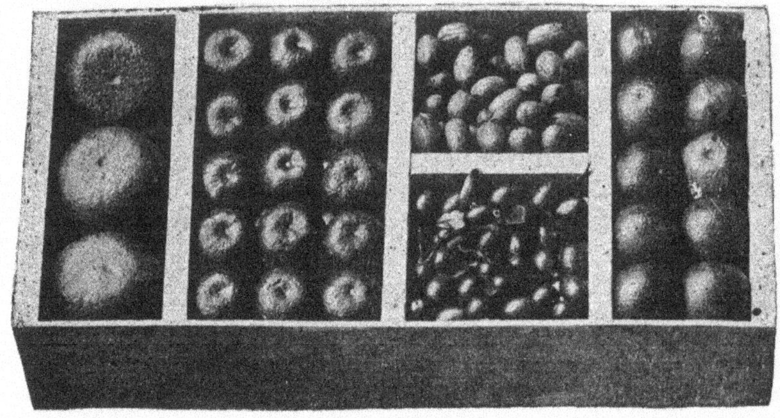

HOLIDAY BOX

One of the regular commercial fancy packs from Rose Farm, Ocean Springs, containing a very carefully selected quality of grapefruit, Satsuma and Creole oranges, kumquat sprays, and fancy large soft shell pecans; the purpose being to give a sample or illustration of the main products of orchards now being so widely developed in this section.   Such other products, as persimmons, can not be shipped in packs of this character.

HANDSOME RESIDENCE OF A. J. CATCHOT, SUPERINTENDENT OF BRIDGES AND BUILDINGS OF THE L. & N. RAILROAD

GRAPE FRUIT

Grape fruit is not quite so hardy as the Satsuma orange, and requires some protection from possible frosts.   This protection can be provided by banking the roots of the trees with dirt, straw or otherwise shielding.   This requires some labor in the fall; the profits well warrant it.   The trees are planted the same as oranges, 134 to 200 to the acre.   Four or five year-old trees will produce more than 100 fruits each season.

Views of the famous "Manyoaks," the handsome Ocean Springs home of Mr. and Mrs. John B. Honor, of New Orleans.

OFFICE OF THE OCEAN SPRINGS NEWS
Write for a sample copy of the paper. Any information cheerfully furnished

LOOKING DOWN PORTER AVENUE

The oaks in Ocean Springs are among the most beautiful in the country, and furnish lovely vistas in every direction.

This picture shows the O'Keefe Stables and the handsome O'Keefe house.   To the old residents of Ocean Springs, the name O'Keefe is one of the traditions of the place.   For over half a century the stables have been in operation.   As the years passed, improvements came, and now luxurious limosines are taking the place of the original teams.

There are fifty-eight automobiles in Ocean Springs, among which the O'Keefe machines are the finest.

OCEAN SPRINGS, A GOOD PLACE TO LIVE

LOCATION: Jackson County, Mississippi, on the Gulf of Mexico. Fifty-two miles west of Mobile, and eighty-two miles east of New Orleans. Transportation facilities are unexcelled, and the L. & N. Railroad affords speedy and practical connection with the markets for orchard products, truck, or other articles of export.

SOCIAL CONDITIONS: Population, 2,000. A winter and summer resort. The citizenship of good manners and good morals renders Ocean Springs a model community. There is no den of vice here, and the history of Ocean Springs is almost unique for the absence of any race antagonism or crime.

CHURCHES; Catholic, Baptist, Methodist, Presbyterian, Episcopal.

CLUBS: Bridge, Civic Federation, Five Hundred, Fortnightly, Home Makers, Maids and Matrons, Mothers. Gulf Coast Citrus Exchange, Country Club, Red Cross Society.

FRATERNAL ORDERS: Masons, Eastern Star, Woodmen, Maccabees, Knights of Columbus, Woodmen Circle, Craftsmen, United Daughters of the Confederacy, Knights of Pythias, Volunteer Fire Company, Hook and Ladder Company.

NEWSPAPER: The Ocean Springs News; All Home Print, linotype.

AMUSEMENTS: Boating, fishing, hunting, picture show. The beautiful days of winter afford the automobilist opportunity for delightful drives along the beach front shell roads that radiate from Ocean Springs fifty miles and more, leading around the Back Bay through Biloxi, down the beach passing the historic home of Jefferson Davis. Golf at the Country Club on a links entirely surrounded by orange and pecan orchards, three miles from town.

GOVERNMENT: An incorporated town, governed by a Mayor and Board of Aldermen.

PUBLIC SCHOOLS: A fine graded school, which has been affiliated so that the graduates can enter college without entrance examination.

MODERN IMPROVEMENTS: Electric lights; modern fire fighting apparatus including a power engine; two volunteer fire companies; artesian water, the cheapest in the United States.; city park; shell roads.

PRINCIPAL PRODUCTS: Lumber, timber, paper shell pecans, oranges, grapefruit, persimmons, pears, corn, hay, sugar cane, oats, rice, peas, potatoes and truck of all kinds and nursery stock. Pulp, paper, fish and oysters, etc. Sheep, hogs and cattle. Business of the county aggregates about $15,000,000.00. Because of the warmth resulting from the water frontage, this region is especially adapted to orchard fruits in general and orange culture in particular. The fact that green stuff can be raised every day in the year, suggests possibilities in the cattle industry.

HEALTH: The highest coastal point between Rockport, Texas, and Mobile, Ala., (elevation, 21:2ft.) Ocean Springs lies on a number of hills that give it a natural drainage and are responsible for the healthy conditions here. A natural cure for hay fever; free of malaria, and a panacea for consumption, asthma, catarrh, neuralgia, rheumatism, and chronic intestinal troubles.

PROSPERITY RECORD: For five consecutive years there have been no tax sales in Ocean Springs. This is believed to be a record.

OCEAN SPRINGS, A GOOD PLACE
TO MAKE A LIVING

CLIMATE: The Government figures show the Monthly and Annual Mean Temperatures here to be as follows: January, 51 degrees, F,; February, 53; March, 57; April, 67; May, 75; June, 80; July, 82; August, 82; September, 78; October, 69; November, 60; December, 51 —General Average, 67.

That this region is warmer than California, is proved by the following figures. The statistics regarding Los Angeles are furnished by the United States Government; those about Ocean Springs, were compiled by The Ocean Springs News. Both are for January, 1916.

Jan.	Ocean Springs	Los Angeles	Jan.	Ocean Springs	Los Angeles
1	64-74	42-46	17	62-66	45-59
2	66-74	46-56	18	30-38	45-59
3	70-74	46-60	19	28-42	44-51
4	60-76	49-54	20	32-52	41-59
5	46-72	49-58	21	52-70	45-58
6	64-76	43-59	22	63-76	47-64
7	64-70	41-64	23	66-70	49-56
8	70-80	45-61	24	50-70	49-56
9	52-60	48-56	25	50-70	51-58
10	57-64	42-55	26	52-70	46-57
11	66-72	40-55	27	65-70	46-58
12	66-76	38-55	28	50-70	44-54
13	72-72	41-57	29	62-70	39-49
14	46-54	51-59	30	65-70	39-56
15	30-56	51-57	31	65-74	38-56
16	52-66	55-60			

PRECIPITATION: The mean annual rainfall in various states is given as follows in government reports: Arizona 5.5 inches; California, 17.3; Florida, 57.9; Illinois, 37.4; Indiana, 34.3; Iowa, 32.9; Ohio, 35.9; Oklahoma, 29.2; Wyoming, 29.3; **Mississippi Coast, 62.3.** California, therefore, with its scant rainfall, necessitating irrigation, is the rich man's country; and Florida, which is the nearest to this region in precipitation, (59.9 inches as against 62.3) has a rainy and dry season. Nearly half of Florida's rain falls in June, July and August; whereas the precipitation is uniform here—being 17.03 inches in winter, 13,29 in spring, 19.74 in summer and 12.32 in autumn.

SOIL: The soil in general is a black to dark brown, sandy loam, fertile with humus and filled with a high content of organic matter from eight inches to three feet in depth, underlaid with a soft clay subsoil and covered with a thrifty growth of native grasses, and responds to kind treatment more rapidly than most any other character of soil and will retain fertilization for years. It is easily worked and does not become baked or muddy; it is just fertile, mellow land, with just enough sand in it to keep it loose and prevent its becoming sticky, when wet. The latest improved farming machinery can be used, and the soil can be worked from 20 to 48 hours after the heaviest rains.

The Department of Agriculture Tells us Why These Lands Have Never Been Developed, in the Following Words:

"Only a few years ago, this section was considered the frontier. Its whole resource was the pine forests, and the sole occupation of the people was in the woods or in the saw mill, and when the lands were denuded, they were regarded as practically worthless, and were little in demand, except by a few people who drifted in from time to time, from the older farmed sections of the state. Farming was begun in a small way, in conjunction with the regular occupation of the people in the woods and mills, and gradually they forsook the mills and took to farming on a commercial basis, but it has only been in the last few years that development has been sufficient to attract attention. **No Section of he South is better adapted to the growing of truck and vegetables and attention is just now being directed to the possibilities in this direction."**